D1559869

BOOK ANALYSIS

By Hudson Cleveland

The Things They Carried
BY TIM O'BRIEN

Bright
≡Summaries.com

CHARACTER STUDY 37

ANALYSIS 43

FURTHER REFLECTION 51

FURTHER READING 55

TIM O'BRIEN

AMERICAN NOVELIST AND SHORT STORY WRITER

- **Born in Austin, Minnesota in 1946.**
- **Notable works:**
  - *If I Die in a Combat Zone, Box Me Up and Ship Me Home* (1973), autobiographical account
  - *Going After Cacciato* (1978), novel
  - *In the Lake of the Woods* (1994), novel

Influenced by his own personal experiences in the Vietnam War (1955-1975), where he served as an infantryman from 1969 to 1970, Tim O'Brien has written extensively on Vietnam both in fiction and in nonfiction. His reflections on the war – from how it impacted the American social fabric to how it has affected his own psyche even decades after the fact – have received widespread acclaim for their nuance, and for their examinations of what makes a story 'true'.

THE THINGS THEY CARRIED

A SEMI-AUTOBIOGRAPHICAL SERIES OF SHORT STORIES SET DURING THE VIETNAM WAR

- **Genre:** short story collection
- **Reference edition:** O'Brien, T. (1991) *The Things They Carried*. New York: Penguin.
- **1ˢᵗ edition:** 1990
- **Themes:** Vietnam War, 'truth' vs 'fact', suicide, PTSD, memories, camaraderie, loss

The Things They Carried is a collection of interconnected short stories that span multiple decades and settings, but have a centring force in O'Brien's personal connections to Vietnam. While grounded in the factual realities of the war and O'Brien's experiences, the stories are also partly fictionalised: an important distinction throughout the collection is between 'story-truth' and 'happening-truth'. Happening-truth comprises objective chronological events, while story-truth focuses more on the psychological reality of those events for O'Brien and others involved in the Vietnam War.

SUMMARY

THE THINGS THEY CARRIED

First Lieutenant Jimmy Cross and his platoon march endlessly across Vietnam. As the title of the story suggests, the focus is on what all the soldiers carry: not only their physical gear, but also their emotional and psychological burdens.

The episode centres primarily on Jimmy Cross, who finds himself trapped in an unrequited love with a girl named Martha. His thoughts are frequently preoccupied with her – he carries thoughts of her as a burden – to the point where it affects his ability to lead his platoon. We are repeatedly told of Ted Lavender when the platoon is described, and are constantly reminded that he is to be killed in a later part of the story. When this does finally occur, Jimmy Cross comes to a certain understanding within himself. He thinks it his fault that Ted Lavender was shot, since he was thinking not of his men but of Martha. After a night of crying, he decides the following morning that he in fact loves and hates Martha, and burns a photograph he had of her. From then on, he decides to be a stricter Lieutenant, and to bring his platoon in line.

NOTES

The narrator, Tim O'Brien, details his time spent talking with Jimmy Cross several years after the war. After some drinks, Jimmy Cross talks about how he met Martha again at a high school reunion, and while he still loved her, she rejected him. However, she gave him a replacement photograph for the one he burned.

SPIN

Tim O'Brien reflects on how memories of the war replay constantly in his head. Most significant is the "bad stuff [that] never stops happening [...] replaying itself over and over" (p. 36), but what is often more frequent are the "odd little fragments that have no beginning and no end" (p. 39).

ON THE RAINY RIVER

O'Brien tells "one story [he's] never told before" (p. 43) due to the shame it brings him. On 17 June 1968, his draft notice for the Vietnam War arrives in the mail, and, despite thinking himself a brave person just waiting for a moment where his bravery can be tested and affirmed, he finds himself in a crisis of character, a "moral split" (p. 48). He is nearing the end of his high school years, and the idea of fighting a war he morally does not believe in sickens him – he thinks he is being drawn into a combat zone that will destroy his life, if not leave him literally dead. The solution to this is to escape to Canada and draft dodge, a frequent occurrence in the US during the Vietnam War. On the other hand, the idea of leaving behind his life, family and friends in this way – and to leave with them a sense of deep shame for their relation to him – tears him from the 'rational' plan to escape it all. His "emotions went from outrage to terror to bewilderment to guilt to sorrow and then back again to outrage. [He] felt a sickness inside [himself]. Real disease" (p. 49).

Finally, one morning at work, he decides to leave "with no plan" (p. 50). He flees northward, stopping at the Tip Top Lodge in Minnesota, right across the border from Canada. There, he meets the aged and solitary Elroy Berdahl, who manages the Lodge. Over the course of a week's stay, O'Brien helps Berdahl with odd jobs, talking little but seeing the man often.

After a time, Berdahl calculates O'Brien's expenses, but winds up offering to pay him for all services rendered, which O'Brien declines – but Berdahl, apparently perceiving O'Brien's issue by this point, leaves the money in O'Brien's cabin in an envelope labelled with the words 'EMERGENCY FUND.'

On the sixth day, Berdahl takes O'Brien out fishing on the Rainy River, the body of water which acts as the border between the US and Canada. He turns away and, without saying anything, essentially leaves O'Brien to make his decision. O'Brien then realises that, as much as he wants to flee, he physically and emotionally cannot. He sees a hallucination across the river – millions of people from his past and his future. He breaks down crying, after thinking that he "would go to the war – [he] would kill and maybe die – because [he] was embarrassed not to" (p. 62). Berdahl then turns the boat back to Minnesota, and the next day O'Brien returns home.

ENEMIES

Two soldiers, Lee Strunk and Dave Jensen, get into a fistfight. Jensen beats Strunk so handily that he gets sent to the hospital to have his nose repaired. When he returns, Jensen grows paranoid that he has a new enemy, imagining that Strunk is now out to get him. Eventually he seems to break down, firing his gun into the air while shouting Strunk's name before sitting on his own for two or three hours straight. That night, he breaks his own nose, and asks Strunk if things are now even – Strunk says yes, then the next morning "couldn't stop laughing" (p. 68) over the smallness of what started it: he had stolen Jensen's jackknife.

FRIENDS

Strunk and Jensen have learned to trust each other, and decide to make a pact between them stating that if either of them gets a wound that makes them unable to walk, the other will kill them. A few months later, Strunk has his leg taken off by a landmine, and begs Jensen not to kill him. Jensen says that he will not and that his leg could likely be sewn back on. The soldiers later hear that Strunk died while on the helicopter out, "which seemed to relieve Dave Jensen of an enormous weight" (p. 72).

HOW TO TELL A TRUE WAR STORY

Bob 'Rat' Kiley's friend, Curt Lemon, dies. Kiley writes his sister a long letter about Lemon, but when she does not write back, he gets angry at her.

O'Brien intersperses fragmented stories of Vietnam with similarly fragmented pedagogical excerpts of what makes war stories true: "A true war story is never moral. [...] There is no virtue. [...] you can tell a true war story by its absolute and uncompromising allegiance to evil" (p. 76).

O'Brien details Curt Lemon's death. Lemon and Kiley were playing with a smoke grenade when Lemon stepped on a rigged 105 shell and died instantly.

The truth of a war story does not necessarily need to be factual – O'Brien's details often seem fantastical, or are undercut by him blatantly saying afterward that certain parts were made up or altered. He relates a story he heard from Mitchell Sanders of a patrol that was ordered to spend a week listening to enemy movement. The group, in the deep mist of a mountainside and their own quiet, begins to hear things. Eventually, they order a bombing on noises that do not even make sense being there, music and voices "like at a cocktail party" (p. 81). They do not tell their superior why they ordered a bombing. "You can tell a true war story," O'Brien says, "by the way it never seems to end" (p. 83).

Sanders comes the following morning to say that the sounds he said the patrol heard were made up, but that they did hear things. O'Brien asks what the moral of the story was, then, and Sanders says that the quiet of Vietnam is his answer.

After Curt Lemon's death, the soldiers find a baby water buffalo. Kiley shoots it over and over again in non-lethal areas, until it is near death, before walking away crying.

"Often in a true war story," O'Brien says, "there is not even a point" (p. 88).

THE DENTIST

O'Brien tells a story about Curt Lemon to "guard against" getting "sentimental about the dead" (p. 95). Lemon, who was infamous for his boastful nature, harboured a deep fear of the dentist.

When one came to perform minor repair work for everyone, Lemon fainted before the dental work even began. Afterward, he insisted that he had a toothache, persisting until he convinced the dentist to pull out "a perfectly good tooth" (p. 97). This appeared, strangely, to placate Lemon.

SWEETHEART OF THE SONG TRA BONG

Rat Kiley tells a story which he vehemently insists is true, despite his penchant for exaggeration. During his time as a medic in the mountains near Tra Bong, an easygoing area in the context of the war, another medic named Mark Fossie claimed that a soldier could in fact bring their girlfriend to Vietnam if they so desired. So, Fossie does: Mary Anne Bell arrives six weeks later.

The couple are "almost disgusting[ly]" (p. 106) romantic. Mary Anne seems at first to be a typical, naive American teenage girl, but she quickly grows curious about her surroundings. She pushes more and more to explore the surrounding area and starts to adopt the style and mannerisms of soldiers. One night, she leaves and does not return. Fossie checks with Rat that she has not been sleeping with any of the other medics, nor that she is in the perimeter of the camp. They cannot find her. The following morning, she returns from 'ambush' with the Green Berets who were stationed at the camp apart from the medics.

Fossie angrily insists on talking to Mary Anne, and afterward things return to a semblance of normality: the couple see each other all the time, and Mary Anne dresses in her civilian garb again. But there is "a strained [...] quality to the way they treated each other" (p. 114), and after Fossie arranges to send her home, Mary Anne grows despondent before disappearing with the Green Berets yet again. This time, she does not return for three weeks.

Fossie goes to the Green Berets' tent to confront her. Rat and another medic, Eddie Diamond, follow and observe. Inside, the tent is "like an animal's den, a mix of blood and scorched hair and excrement and the sweet-sour odor of moldering flesh" (p. 119). Bones are littered everywhere, many of them apparently Vietnamese. Mary Anne wears her American clothes, but also a necklace made of tongues. She says that Fossie does not "know what [Vietnam is] all about" (p. 121).

Rat's story ends there, and he says that the rest is but hearsay — everything before he had witnessed firsthand. Purportedly, "Vietnam had the effect of a powerful drug" (p. 123) on Mary Anne. She began to do things that made even the Green Berets uncomfortable, before vanishing for longer and longer periods of time. After a while, she vanished and never was seen again.

STOCKINGS

O'Brien's platoon simultaneously snickers and marvels at Henry Dobbins' good luck charm: his girlfriend's panties. With them, he has survived multiple situations of almost certain fatality. Even after the couple break up, Dobbins continues to tie them around his neck, stating, "The magic doesn't go away" (p. 130).

CHURCH

The platoon comes across a pagoda inhabited only by two monks. The monks especially like Henry Dobbins, the three having a "quietness they shared" (p. 134). Dobbins one day tells Kiowa that perhaps he will join the monks after the war. This prompts a brief discussion on religion and churches between the two.

THE MAN I KILLED

Tim O'Brien has killed a man. He stares mutely at the body for an indefinite amount of time, but likely for many minutes, if not some hours. The details not only of the gore, but also of the person, are meticulously pictured. O'Brien also ascribes an entire life to the man, hypothesising that he was someone with a distaste for war and love for calculus, only fighting because it was expected, similarly to O'Brien himself. Kiowa attempts to snap O'Brien out of his daze, urging him to talk to him, but O'Brien says nothing.

AMBUSH

O'Brien's daughter, who is nine years old, asks if he has ever killed anyone. He tells her no, but reflects on how he killed the man in the previous story. While O'Brien was on guard during an ambush in My Khe, the man walked by his position. Though "There was no real peril" and "the young man would have passed by" (p. 149), O'Brien lobbed a grenade at him, killing him.

STYLE

The platoon comes across a girl dancing in front of a burned-down hamlet. Inside a house they find her family dead and burned. Azar does not understand her dancing, and later that night mocks it. Henry Dobbins then carries him over to a well and says that if he does not want to be dropped in, he needs to "dance right" (p. 154).

SPEAKING OF COURAGE

Norman Bowker, home from the war, drives around the lake in his home town over and over again in his father's Chevy. He imagines telling three people the story of how he almost won a Silver Star medal: his father, his one-time girlfriend Sally Kramer, and his friend Max Arnold, who drowned in the lake prior to the war.

The story he wanted to tell but never did was that once he and his platoon camped out on a 'shit field' – literally, a field where the locals defecate, and have done so for generations, creating a viscerally odorous atmosphere. While out on this field, they come under enemy mortar fire. This essentially turns the field into faecal quicksand, and, caught in the open, the platoon has to hide in the slime. Norman notices that Kiowa has begun to be sucked under, and tries to save him, but backs off due to the smell. "Courage was not always a matter of yes or no," he thinks in his imagined telling of the story. "Sometimes you were very brave up to a point and then beyond that point you were not so brave" (p. 166).

NOTES

O'Brien reflects on Bowker's story. Bowker had committed suicide in 1978, three years after suggesting the story to O'Brien through a long personal letter. After a few iterations, the story appeared in an anthology, but Bowker seemed disappointed by it. After Bowker's suicide, O'Brien heavily revised the story to include the 'shit field' itself, as well as Bowker's real name. O'Brien insists, however, that Bowker did not lose his nerve or the Silver Star for valour in the field: "That part of the story [was O'Brien's] own" (p. 182).

IN THE FIELD

The platoon returns to the field to search for Kiowa's body in the rain. Two more people internally express their guilt at the situation: First Lieutenant Jimmy Cross for not moving them to a more suitable position, and an unnamed soldier for turning on his flashlight in the night to show Kiowa a picture and thus giving away their location.

Mitchell Sanders blames Jimmy Cross entirely for Kiowa's death, considering the 'shit field' to be an obvious tactical mistake. As they all search for the body, Azar cracks jokes, much to the chagrin of Sanders and Norman Bowker. Jimmy Cross composes a letter to Kiowa's family in his head, while half-heartedly assisting the frantic, nameless soldier.

While Jimmy Cross and the nameless soldier search in the field – Cross for Kiowa, but the soldier for the picture of his girlfriend he had been showing Kiowa – the rest of the platoon finds the body. After a significant amount of time and effort are spent unearthing him from the muck, they call in a helicopter to take him away. Jimmy Cross lays in the mud, and imagines that he is back home.

GOOD FORM

O'Brien explains the difference between 'story-truth' and 'happening-truth,' and says that the two can be contradictory yet simultaneously real. "I want you to feel what I felt," he claims. "I want you to know why story-truth is truer sometimes than happening-truth" (p. 203).

FIELD TRIP

O'Brien returns 20 years later to the field where Kiowa died, with his ten-year-old daughter Kathleen. Their trip through Vietnam is his way of "offering a small piece of her father's history" (p. 208), but she unsurprisingly seems to have trouble grasping the gravity of the situation: "The war was as remote to her as cavemen and dinosaurs" (*ibid.*).

O'Brien finds the spot where he thinks Mitchell Sanders had come across Kiowa's rucksack. He wades into the water with Kiowa's moccasins, and wedges them into the ground below. He tries to say something of import, but can think of nothing.

THE GHOST SOLDIERS

O'Brien thinks back to the two times he had been shot. The first time, Rat Kiley dealt with the wound professionally and easily, and O'Brien quickly recovered. The second time, Rat Kiley himself had been wounded and replaced by Bobby Jorgenson, a fresh-faced medic nervous about being out in the field for the first time. He botched O'Brien's wound, which forced him to spend several months recovering.

During his convalescence, O'Brien can hardly sleep due to the pain. He harbours a deep resentment for Jorgenson, wanting him to "feel exactly what [O'Brien] felt" (p. 220).

O'Brien's Company comes in for 'stand-down' and O'Brien catches up with them. Another soldier, Morty Phillips, had "used up his luck" (p. 221) and died not in battle, but from a disease he caught from swimming in a river. After his several months' absence, O'Brien feels a distance with Alpha Company, tempered by his 'civilian' life and their continued fraternity in the field.

Jorgenson comes to apologise to O'Brien, and O'Brien "hate[s] him for making [O'Brien] stop hating him" (p. 227). He does not forgive him. He decides to give Jorgenson 'consequences' for almost killing him. He tries to enlist Mitchell Sanders, who refuses, and then Azar, who accepts.

Azar's excitement about the operation almost makes O'Brien cancel it. But when O'Brien sees Jorgenson at dinner happily fraternising with the Company, his resolve hardens.

While Jorgenson is on watch, O'Brien and Azar set up various noisemakers and visual effects to psychologically terrorise him over the course of the night. They do this slowly and for hours, and O'Brien watches the effects, satisfied. Azar decides to take it a step further, however, despite O'Brien's insistence that "the score was even" (p. 237). Azar claims to love things like this, replications of the war.

The next step shatters the illusion, however, and Jorgenson realises that he has been played. Azar leaves the horrified O'Brien behind, but not before kicking him in the head. Jorgenson takes him to patch him up, where the two tentatively agree that they are even.

NIGHT LIFE

O'Brien tells how Rat Kiley got hurt. During a period when, out of concern for enemies in the area, the platoon slept during the day and moved only at night, the psychological toll weighed heavily on everyone. For Rat, though, it became too much to bear. After a week, he went from completely quiet to constantly talking. He talked about unusual things, such as all the bugs in Vietnam being out to get him, and picked up unusual habits. After another week, he confessed to Mitchell Sanders that he was constantly picturing the members of the platoon dead whenever he looked at them, in grisly detail. Shortly after, he shot himself in the foot and was sent away.

THE LIVES OF THE DEAD

O'Brien talks about how "stories can save us" by allowing the dead to "smile and sit up and return to the world" (p. 256). He uses two examples. The first is from the first dead body he saw while in Vietnam: when the platoon found it, they all shook its hand with a strange 'formality,' "like a funeral without the sadness" (p. 257). This leads to another, the first death he actually witnessed: the love of his life at nine years old, Linda.

O'Brien describes an often wordless but nonetheless true and real love between him and Linda. The two once went on a 'double date' with O'Brien's parents to a film, on the way to which O'Brien commented positively on her new red cap.

Linda began wearing her new cap all the time, until one day during class another boy lifted it off her, revealing her bald and scarified head. O'Brien, in their quiet way, said wordlessly to her "*Sure, okay*" (p. 264). Linda died some months later of a brain tumour. O'Brien "as a writer now [... wants] to save Linda's life. Not her body – her life" (p. 265). At the age of nine, he began to have vivid, controlled dreams about her, a way "of making the dead seem not quite so dead" (p. 267) that he rediscovered in Vietnam with all his friends who were killed.

When he was ten, O'Brien asked his father to go see Linda's body in state. The body, completely different from when she was alive and most certainly dead, shattered somewhat the illusion of aliveness he had built in his head. But he is able to attain the same effect through writing his stories.

CHARACTER STUDY

TIM O'BRIEN

O'Brien first began grappling with the concept of Vietnam when he received his draft notice in 1968. From then, he claims writing stories is not necessarily therapeutic, but a method of separating himself from the war, of legitimising and categorising his experiences by a distance that renders them more understandable.

O'Brien, save for the stories where he features as the main character, frequently goes unmentioned throughout the text, instead narrating from a third-person distance.

O'Brien's feelings toward the Vietnam War as a whole are incredibly complex, though his relationships with friends and family remain more or less positive throughout his decades-long reflections.

FIRST LIEUTENANT JIMMY CROSS

The leader of O'Brien's platoon, Cross harbours an unrequited love for a girl at home named Martha. Whenever men in his platoon are killed, he tends to feel personally responsible for their deaths – even when other members of the platoon seem to think it was their fault.

HENRY DOBBINS

The heavy machine-gunner of the platoon due to his large frame, Dobbins has a gentle nature. He carries his girlfriend's panties around his neck as a good-luck charm.

DAVE JENSEN

Though he appears in a primary role only once, Jensen's story with Lee Strunk encapsulates the paranoia of finding oneself without friends in a country full of enemies.

TED LAVENDER

Lavender, always scared, took tranquilisers every day to 'mellow' himself. His death, which is mentioned before it is actually described, is not only significant to Jimmy Cross, but to O'Brien's understanding of life and death in Vietnam.

MITCHELL SANDERS

Sanders often listens to stories that the other soldiers tell, and always wonders what their 'moral' is. He grows frustrated with Cross' leadership, particularly after the death of Kiowa, and himself acts as a centring force for the platoon due to his measure and trustworthiness.

NORMAN BOWKER

O'Brien utilises Bowker's story of his life back home after the war, related to him through personal letters, as emblematic of those interminably tied to their experiences in wartime.

BOB "RAT" KILEY

The platoon medic, Rat Kiley has a penchant for telling stories with outlandishly exaggerated details. Despite this, O'Brien casts his storytelling type as one that, while surpassing the reality of the actual events, nonetheless remains true to the 'feeling' the story invokes in those who lived it.

KIOWA

Kiowa always carries an illustrated copy of the New Testament. A devout Baptist, he is also a Native American. A close friend of O'Brien's, his death weighs heavily in the collective narrative, elaborated over the course of three consecutive stories.

AZAR

Azar constantly uses dark humour to blunt the horrors of the war. Many in the platoon dislike him for this lack of sincerity, which often borders on cruelty. At the death of Kiowa, however, he does show sentimentality.

ELROY BERDAHL

Elroy is an old man living in solitude near the US-Canada border. O'Brien relies on his quiet and reserved nature as an anchor during

KATHLEEN O'BRIEN

Kathleen is O'Brien's daughter, to whom he tries to explain his experiences. Her innocence as a child forces him to come to terms with Vietnam in new ways.

MARK FOSSIE

A member of Rat Kiley's older platoon, Fossie helicopters his girlfriend in to Vietnam, only to lose her to the war's hypnotic violence.

ANALYSIS

'HAPPENING-TRUTH' AND 'STORY-TRUTH'

The core dichotomy running through every story in O'Brien's collection is between events as they actually occur, and events as they imprint themselves on the minds of those who witness them. He calls the former 'happening-truth' and the latter 'story-truth'. "Story-truth," he says, "is truer sometimes than happening-truth" (p. 203).

The two, however, are not mutually exclusive, nor does there seem to be only one of them for each story told. When Kathleen O'Brien asks her father whether he has killed anyone, he can *simultaneously* say with honesty 'yes' and 'no', for story-truth does not negate the actual events, or vice versa. The two exist inextricably together, for only the bare facts cover 'happening-truth': O'Brien is "forty-three years old, [...] a writer now, and a long time ago [he] walked through Quang Ngai Province as a foot soldier", but "Almost everything else is invented" (*ibid.*).

This is the reason so many single stories are re-turned to in entirely new ways. The preeminent example of this is the story of Kiowa's death: it becomes the central subject matter of "Speaking of Courage", "Notes", "In the Field", and "Field Trip". Yet, in each one, Kiowa's death means entirely different things for different people, and indeed the fault of his death rests on different people. In "Speaking of Courage", Norman Bowker blames himself for being unable to save Kiowa from sinking into the field, though O'Brien in his narrative authority clears him from any wrongdoing and responsibility in "Notes". In "Notes", the impression Kiowa's death made on Bowker seemed in part to lead to his suicide later in life. Yet, in "In the Field", the blame shifts again. Jimmy Cross puts the onus of Kiowa's death on himself, not only due to his general duty as platoon leader, but also for his lack of tactical awareness in not deciding to move away from the dangerously open field in the first place, leaving the platoon open to attack. Simultaneously, the nameless soldier who was showing Kiowa a picture blames himself, thinking that shining his flashlight painted a target on the platoon's position for mortar fire. Over all these, as well, is the general sense that it was "the War" that was to blame, with its unpredictable and dispassionate taking of human life. And, further, O'Brien later in "Field Trip" thinks of the field as the place where he had "swallowed" his "belief in [himself as a man of some small dignity and courage" (p. 210), suggesting if not a vague sense of blame towards himself, then a blame of the field or Vietnam itself for taking the "person [he] had once been" (*ibid.*).

Despite all these conflicting testimonies, the goal of lining them up in sequence seems not to be for the readers to judge which is the truest and disregard the others – but to realise that they are all simultaneously true, regardless of the paradoxes. This is one of the defining aspects of Vietnam in the American consciousness: it fragmented the mind, collapsing the simple 'true-false' binary.

WOMEN BEYOND THE WAR

Women have for a long time occupied a strange place not only in wartime, but in literature. Typical femininity denotes dependence on a masculine figure, or a divine female figure upon which the masculine looks as an object (emphasis on object, as opposed to person) of desire. But in *The Things They Carried*, images of the feminine are complicated. While many of the men carry mementos of women they love or hold affections for, very few of these mementos are of women who actually reciprocate those emotions. Jimmy Cross, Henry Dobbins and the nameless soldier all carry photographs (or, in Dobbins' case, panties) of women who do not love them back. Even O'Brien himself carries in memory Linda, the girl he loved when he was nine years old and who died of brain cancer. Another prominent female figure is Mary Anne in "Sweetheart of the Song Tra Bong," the naïve but curious and quick-learning teenager who 'goes primal' as she forsakes her home of America and loses herself in the Vietnamese mountains.

All of these female figures, while still not given a prominent voice of their own, nonetheless tend to eschew archetypal femininity: those who are objects of male love do not love back simply by virtue of the soldiers' participation in the war, and those who come to Vietnam and start off with a protected status soon become more gruesome than even the most sadistic of American soldiers.

TIME

O'Brien's earliest longform recollection is when he is nine years old, when his love for Linda began, and his latest is in the present day (that is, at the time of writing, when he was aged 43). There exists no real linear chronology: his romantic endeavours with Linda are told in the final story, "The Lives of the Dead", and the first story, "The Things They Carried", begins in the very middle of the Vietnam War.

That first story acts as a useful analogue to considerations of time and temporality by those who experienced the Vietnam War. While "the things they carried were largely determined by necessity" (p. 4), O'Brien also enumerates all the things they carry of more abstract value, such as fear, bravery, superstitions, memories, and so on. There is no real order to the listing of what they carried, only what seems to arise almost naturally. Similarly, the order of the story collection seems to be ordered by that automatic selection, by one story that brings up the idea of another instance of fear, or superstition, or a similar memory or person or thing.

One of O'Brien's primary motifs is this sense of the fragmentation and disordering of time, stories that are "odd little fragments that have no beginning and no end" (p. 39). "You can tell a true war story," O'Brien says, "by the way it never seems to end. Not then, not ever" (p. 83). Deaths such as those of Ted Lavender, Curt Lemon, and Kiowa replay or remain in stasis seemingly forever: they do not form linear narratives, but freeze-frames in time that can be revisited over and over.

This jumbled sense of time, while one of O'Brien's most important motifs, is also one of the most difficult to grasp.

FURTHER REFLECTION

SOME QUESTIONS TO THINK ABOUT...

- How are the deaths of O'Brien's close friends dealt with, in contrast to enemy combatants he sees dead and those he kills?
- What is the significance of 'story-truth'? Is it a kind of disingenuous embellishment, or does it add an authenticity to O'Brien's stories that would not be there in a straightforwardly factual chronology?
- In the story "On the Rainy River", O'Brien mentions his fear of a deep sense of shame should he dodge the draft. How does 'shame' shape key points in the narrative of the collection as a whole?
- O'Brien often bemoans the difficulty he has in properly relating his experiences during the Vietnam War to anyone who was not in it. What are some of the unique psychological experiences of O'Brien and his fellow soldiers in the text, and how do they contrast with those who do not seem to understand the

psychological impact of the war?

- The platoons frequently use dark humour and metonymy (the use of one word as a substitute for another, more straightforward one – for example, when O'Brien refers to corpses instead as 'kicked buckets') to soften the death and horrors of the war. In what ways do these tactics seem to help the soldiers? In what ways do they hurt?

- How does the sequence in which the stories are placed compare to the chronological order of the stories? Is there any significance in ordering the stories non-linearly?

- In what ways is the Vietnam War intergenerational in its aftereffects, as presented in the novel?

- Though the Vietnam War undoubtedly had a massive impact on many Americans and American society as a whole, Vietnam itself suffered far more collateral damage, with hundreds of thousands more civilians and soldiers estimated dead than the total number of lost US soldiers. Does O'Brien's American-centric account in any way problematise representations of Vietnam?

- What role do women play in this collection of short stories?

We want to hear from you!
Leave a comment on your online library
and share your favourite books on social media!

FURTHER READING

REFERENCE EDITION

- O'Brien, T. (1991) *The Things They Carried*. New York: Penguin.

www.brightsummaries.com

Ebook EAN: 9782808019071

Paperback EAN: 9782808019088

Legal Deposit: D/2019/12603/120

Cover: © Primento

Digital conception by Primento, the digital partner of
publishers.